Imagine You!

40 Days of Devotions: Finding Your Identity in God's Image

Created by
Nancy Hulshult and Francesca King

ISBN: 978-1-7354852-6-3

Published by:
NarratusCreative | Narratus Press
P.O. Box 1413
Hamilton, OH 45012

Design: NarratusCreative | narratuscreative.com

Produced in the United States of America

DEDICATION

This book is dedicated to Michael Dantley, for his inspiring study and preaching of God's Word, for his mentorship, and for his love of God's people.

Thanks to Debbie Day and Sheryl Burk, for their help, honest feedback and encouragement.

Thanks to Nancy's husband, Darrell Hulshult, for his inspiring leadership and partnership in ministry. Together with God, we are ONE!

Thanks to Francesca's parents, Candace King and Rodney Posey, for their inspiring guidance of Francesca and other young people to follow God's heart.

I would have lost heart, unless I believed that I would see the goodness of the Lord in the land of the living. Wait on the Lord; Be of good courage, and He shall strengthen your heart; Wait, I say on the Lord! (Psalm 27:13-14, NKJV)

Contents

Foreword

In this season of multiple challenges that are bombarding our lives with a ferocity that has almost been unprecedented in our times, we are discovering a genuine need to grapple with and settle the question of who we are. Our identity and the resolution of our investigation of our individual culture is top of mind for many. Innumerable instruments to investigate our inner selves have gained our intense interest. However, to find our answers in the word of God is one sure method to lead to a successful search. For this reason, Hulshult and King's Imagine You! 40 Days of Devotions: Finding Your Identity in God's Image, is a must read. The intergenerational perspectives presented in this devotional have the potential to impact all those who are seriously pursuing the life-changing project of defining themselves and their life's purpose. The very idea of promoting our self-image through the Lord's prescriptions provides us a guide for establishing who we genuinely are.

Imagine You! is a phenomenal way to personalize the reading of the book of Genesis. This forty-day devotional dares to require the reader to come to grips with the salient matters in the first book of the Bible. That grappling personally with the content in these chapters for forty days is greatly enhanced through the devotional process. In fact, the four-step process is an exemplary pedagogical and devotional process. Hulshult and King require the reader to Read, Reflect, Respond and Resolve. In this way, we not only read the word of God, but we are also compelled to internalize and to then strategize how we will operationalize the living word of God. This devotional not only challenges the reader to ponder but to then practice what has percolated through the four-step process.

I commend the authors Nancy Hulshult and Francesca King for the creative and comprehensive way they challenge us to see the utility of God's word in impacting how we see ourselves. Such a timely devotional for a season when it is most needed. Embrace this devotional with the commitment to see it impact your life in a phenomenal way.

Michael E. Dantley, Ed.D.
Bishop and Senior Pastor
Christ Emmanuel Christian Fellowship
Cincinnati, Ohio

Introduction

by Nancy Hulshult

God draws people together who would normally never cross paths. That is how it was with Francesca and me. I was watching a Tuesday night online Bible study when the leader, Bishop Michael Dantley, announced a special program on the upcoming Friday. Several young ministers-in-training would share their thoughts about the future of the church post-pandemic. I can't describe exactly what went through my mind, but my spirit was compelled to connect with a young woman of the group. My husband was in agreement. I emailed my intentions to Bishop Dantley that I wanted to "pay it forward" out of gratitude for all the times that I was given financial and spiritual support in the seminary and in my educational career.

As soon as I heard Francesca speak of the importance of authenticity in ministry, I understood why God had led me to her. From our first text and then our first phone call, we both knew that the Lord was working in our lives. Francesca is studying to be a music teacher and youth pastor, and I am a retired school principal and active minister. We both love to play piano and plink around on ukuleles. She loves to write beautiful spiritual songs, and I love to write about spiritual happenings. We both love the book of Genesis and all the ways that we learn about humanity, God, and our relationships in these first chapters of the Bible.

Somewhere in our weekly chats, we decided to camp out

in Genesis and record our reflections and responses, which turned into 40 days of devotions. We were interested to learn how we would process Genesis from our perspectives. Francesca is a black woman in her mid-20's, and I am a white woman in my mid-60's. With our age and cultural differences, would God speak to us in different ways, or would we interpret God's creation and redemption story in the same way? After all, the Bible says that we are all created in God's image.

Genesis Chapter 1, verse 26 says:

> Then God said, "Let us make mankind in our image, in our likeness, so that they may rule over the fish in the sea and the birds in the sky, over the livestock and all the wild animals, and over all the creatures that move along the ground."

From the first chapter in Genesis, Francesca and I agree that the plural pronouns in the phrases "let us" and "in our image, in our likeness" confirm that both of us are created in God's image. The plurality of the reality tells us that neither she nor I nor you, the reader, are created more like God than another. Adam and Eve were created in different genders for the purpose of continuing humankind, but they both have the DNA of our Creator and our God, the God of Genesis. That puts us all on an equal footing in our relationship with God the Creator, God the Savior Jesus, and God the Holy Spirit.

The structure of our devotional book has four parts:

Read a quick summary of parts of each chapter that captured our attention. We listed chapters and verses with the summary, in case you are the type of reader who does not want to read your Bible as you read and pray using a devotional. If you wish, you can read the entire chapter(s) from your Bible before reading our reflections.

Our reflections about Scripture that interface with the chapters or verses.

Our responsive questions as related to our lives as a result of our reflections.

A place to reflect, to answer the responsive questions, or to make conscious decisions to do or think differently as a result of the day's devotion.

In preparation for this devotional study, we did not conduct research, study particular theologians, or ask other people for their thoughts before we encountered Scripture and recorded our reflections. We didn't need to come to an agreement; we just added our thoughts. As we verbally processed together, we shared many self-revelations. At times, we knew that we were "preaching to ourselves" as we explained what God was telling us about our own personal situations and challenges. At the conclusion of our 40-day study in Genesis, we found a renewed sense of our identity as created human beings by God, who loves us, who forgives us for our mistakes, and who wants to stay in a close relationship with us.

Now we invite you to join us. If you wish, you can invite others to join us as a part of your small group of friends who love to read Scripture and talk about it together.

Francesca's reflections are marked with an 'F';

Nancy's reflections are marked with an 'N'.

We have added self-reflective questions and space for you to respond to our reflections, to add yours, and to write your resolve for any questions that pique your particular interest. Join us in our fascination and respect for the book of Genesis: the story where the world began...the history where we all began in God's image.

Day 1

read

Genesis Chapters 1 & 2

HIGHLIGHTED TEXT:

- 1:4 God saw that the light was good.
- 1:10 God noted that the seas were good.
- 1:12 God saw that the vegetation was good.
- 1:18 God saw that the two great lights (day and night) were good.
- 1:21 God saw that the sea creatures and winged creatures were good
- 1:25 God saw that the animals moving along the ground were good.
- 1:31 God created man and woman and saw "all that he had made, and it was very good."
- 1:26 "Let us make man in our image, in our likeness..."
- 2:1-3 God "rested" on the seventh day.
- 2:2-3 says that God finished all his work, rested, and "blessed the seventh day, and made it holy, because on it he rested from all the work of creating that he had done."
- 2:9 says that in the middle of the garden were the tree of life and the tree of the knowledge of good and evil.
- 2:16 And the Lord God commanded the man, "You are free to eat from any tree in the garden;
- 2:19 (God) brought them to the man to see what he would name them, and whatever the man called each living creature, that was its name.
- 2:25 says that originally the man and his wife were both naked, and they felt no shame.

reflect

As God created, He reflected on each type of creation and assessed every one, and He noted that they were good creations. To be made in God's image is for us to be able to reason, to love, to appreciate beauty, to have free will, to make decisions on our own, and to create at a level well above any other created being.

To be created in God's image reminds us of children who look or act exactly like their parents. What is in the parents is in the children. What is in God is in us, except for the capacity to do evil, which was brought on first by Adam and Eve's disobedience, and then by ourselves through our misuse of God's gift of free will. Just as parents want to be proud of their children, God wants to "be proud" of His children who are able to do so much of what God can do, but not entirely on our own, that is, but with the guidance that God's example and Holy Spirit gives us.

Nowhere in the Genesis account of creation do we read that God tried to create something, scratched his head, and then scratched the idea because He didn't like the outcome. Because of his nature of purity and righteousness, God's perfect thoughts became perfect Words, and His Words brought life into being. Because we are human and infected by sin and our humanness, sometimes we tend to act before we fully think through our actions and their consequences. Since we are made in God's likeness, we would fare better to follow God's example: to think with purity of intentions, to speak in truth and with the best of intentions, and then to reflect on the results of our actions, beginning from our thoughts through to their consequences. When we create goodness in the world, then we, like God, can reflect and enjoy the fruits of our work.

God "rested" on the seventh day, but of course, God does not need to rest, as He is limitless in his power and energy. However, not only did he model for us the need to take a break from labor, but also to set aside time to appreciate creation, what has been made! In chapter 1 of Genesis, God had noted that all creation was good, but He set aside time.

Since God never sleeps, this time had to have been devoted to "taking in" his creation, to appreciate it, to watch and study creation, to love His creations by devoting attention to them. That is what we can learn about our seventh day of the week: to rest from work, to meditate on what is before us, appreciate creation around us, and to love creation – from the moon and sun to nature to people.

In Genesis 2, we see that seeking wisdom is one thing; curiosity is another. Knowledge is a 2-edged sword. Who would ever want to know evil? God told only "man", i.e. Adam, the command about not eating from the tree of the knowledge of good and evil. God did not tell Eve directly, so the serpent (Satan) was able to distort and contort the message to tempt Eve. Why would we want to waste our efforts to "know" evil, but the temptation to "know" good, i.e. to "know" what God knows, drew Eve in. Eve did not think of the consequences or repercussions when she first took a bite of the fruit from the forbidden tree.

God allowed Adam to do what God did: say it, and it will be so. In partnership, God permitted Adam the authority to name each living creature. The Lord even brought each one to Adam. Adam just had to sit (or stand) there and decide what its name should be. That's a lot of power and honor from the Creator.

We also call things into our lives by naming them or speaking situations into being. When we try to predict that bad things will happen, many times they do, whether by design or unintentional actions. When we speak positive words to people, we can change how others view themselves, us, or the world. Words have incredible power. God used his Word to let there be light; we need to use our words in the same way with the same creative positive purpose.

Shame entered into us when sin entered us through Eve and Adam.

The Bible begins with emphasis on God working in relationship with creation: everything connecting to other created beings. In order to be fruitful and multiply, everything has to be connected. God was creating a world from something that was empty and broken and had no desire in it. He only wanted to put things that were good in it; everything good from the plants to the fish had to be connected. It's bigger than the circle of life because God was actually creating life.

In Genesis Chapter 1, God has always known that we were going to look at something for what we are supposed to look like. That's why God said, "Let us create man in our own image" because he knew that we were going to try and imagine and look at other people, constantly trying to fill gaps in us that we didn't know were there. Instead of giving us any opportunity to try to create something else, we were created "in our own image" so that we would only create images that he imagined we would create. God wanted us to have an image that we can see in ourselves. We are created "in our own image." He knows that we were always going to be looking at our image. We are only going to reflect what God imagined.

In Genesis Chapter 2, this is the first time that God said something was not good. He says, "It is not good for man to be alone. I will make a helper suitable for him." It is important in the theme of relationship that in order to advance in the kingdom, in order to really put roots down, we have to be connected with somebody who is like minded and progressing toward the same goal.

---

respond

How often am I intentional about thinking, speaking, and doing what would please God and give me joy in behaving in Godly ways?

What am I doing actively to fight sin in my life and in my sphere of influence? What am I doing to live by example and to positively influence others to live a life that shows that we are created in the image of God?

---

resolve

_____

_____

_____

_____

_____

_____

_____

_____

_____

_____

_____

_____

Day 2

read

Genesis Chapters 3 & 4

HIGHLIGHTED TEXT:

- Genesis 3:16 To the woman he said, "...your desire will be for your husband, and he will rule over you." In 3:17, God tells Adam that he will eat of the ground all the days of his life.
- Genesis 3:8 Even adults (Adam and Eve) hide from God when they sin, but the Lord calls to them, "Where are you?" even though God knew where they were.
- Genesis 3:7 and Genesis 3:21 God helps us with redemption and restoration. Adam and Eve covered themselves with leaves in verse 7, but in verse 21, God made garments of skin and clothed them.
- Genesis 3:22 Consequence for sin: God says that "the man has now become one of us, knowing good and evil. He must not be allowed to reach out his hand and take also from the tree of life and eat, and live forever." And God banished Adam and Eve to work the soil, and God guarded the way to the tree of life.
- Genesis 4:7 But if you do not do what is right, sin is crouching at your door; it desires to have you, but you must master it.
- Genesis 4:10 the Lord said, "What have you done? Listen! Your brother's blood cries out to me from the ground.
- Genesis 4:15 Even though God punishes Cain, He protects him. 4:15 Then the Lord put a mark on Cain so

that no one who found him would kill him. 4:16 So Cain went out from the Lord's presence and lived in the land of Nod, east of Eden.
* Genesis 4:25 God restores with another son, Seth, to replace Abel.

reflect

Even before the fall, the instructions from God for Adam and Eve about what not to eat were already made clear, and we see Adam falling for what the enemy sadly had put into his brain. Just telling him not to eat from the tree was a precursor to what happened. Adam and Eve had a desire to have more power than what life is supposed to look like. The fact that God even let Adam name a creature was so much power already. Man was already a part of God's painting and was allowed to put paint on the page, literally helping to draw the painting of the world. Why would he want any more?

We have this image of women being subservient to men, but when we read about the fall, we see that Woman made it like that. Today in the world we see this power struggle, but no one in particular was necessarily supposed to be "in power". God was in power over everything, but when we take our ideas for ourselves, we are taking the reins. However, we are not the only ones who want the reins. We were created to be in partnership, but both Eve and Adam misused their power given to them by their Creator. It was after the fall that God told Woman that her desire will be for her husband, and he will rule over you. God put her in that place because of her actions to disobey God and influence Adam to do the same.

When we see other options of our image in our vision and the way we see ourselves, we see that what we are doing is not reflecting God. We then are taking power from ourselves and are trying to assume the authority in trying to make concessions from what we can't fill in our lives. That is when we get further into sin: addictions, pornography, drugs, and everything that is lustful and for self rather than for the advancement of the kingdom. Then our perception of what we are supposed to do is clouded by our own judgement. That is the problem. We always seek our judgement and wisdom. Our lack of wisdom and judgement comes from not being in tune with God because He always is giving us the path, guiding us with decisions to make. We keep trying to do everything on our own.

We try to create our own painting of our world, which ends up being messed up. We got into animal sacrifices because we can't pay for what we did in our sin against God. God keeps trying to tell us over and over again, "I keep redeeming you. I keep redeeming you," but we keep choosing what we want for ourselves. We are so frustrating to God, but He is so good to continue to redeem us.

The example of Cain and Abel is a reminder of our constant battle against the flesh and our self desires. We are always trying to be accepted when we should know that we have already been accepted by God. Part of the problem is what Cain and Abel's parents did. Their sin has become generational as each generation is looking for what image to reflect. Adam and Eve acted like they did not have an image to reflect. They acted like God didn't say, "Let us create man in our own image and likeness." Man and Woman looked like God and were in God's image. They were the character of Christ in the world, but through the generations, we start to see generational chaos with Lamech and on down. If we are being fulfilled, we wouldn't have to search. Again, Man and Woman continue to search for acceptance when they are already accepted by God. We get stuck in sin and forget that Jesus was sent so that we could receive forgiveness for sin.

From their disobedience in the Garden of Eden, husbands were given authority over wives, and we all became farmers to get our food from the sweat of our brow. If Eve hadn't listened to the serpent, women would have been equal partners with men from the beginning, and we wouldn't be doing any farming or cooking. We would be chomping on delicious food that we didn't have to grow or prepare. Pass the salt, Honey!

God had a plan for us in a beautiful garden that satisfied all our needs without working for them. Adam and Eve, and all of us, could have eaten from the Tree of Life and lived forever, except for our desire for knowledge and equality with God. The Garden of Eden offered all that was good, innocent, and protected, so why did Adam and Eve have to disobey and thirst for more knowledge, including that of Evil? Why couldn't we have stayed content in the garden with the just the knowledge of all things Good? Eating from the Tree of the Knowledge of Good and Evil was forbidden, which is understandable in the best interests for Adam and Eve. Although we may be insatiably curious, who of us ever really wants to know the dark side of life, once we see it, experience it, and understand its consequences?

Consider the power of technology today. Parents and schools give our children access to learn so many good things about the world, but also children can gain access to so many dark and dangerous and evil things of the world. Parents set rules for their children regarding computers, but children of all ages either find a way around the restrictions or receive uninvited pop-ups that steal their attention and innocence. Children used to be exposed to "the world" when they left home as young adults. Now they are exposed as young as toddlers.

Adults are just as vulnerable, as evidenced by the high number of addictions to pornography that has ruined marriages, careers, and lives of adults of all ages and all levels of spirituality. Just as Adam and Eve had their eyes opened to Evil and suffered drastic consequences, so also do our children suffer from the consequences of overexposure to all the temptations and evil of the world.

God was calling Adam and Eve to account for their actions and distance from Him. In our sins today, we are tempted to hide from our wrongdoings, but God seeks us through His Holy Spirit to convict us to repent and turn back to him. He is always calling us to wholeness in Him.

God helped Adam and Eve in their recovery process. To make garments of animal skin, God had to sacrifice the blood of the animal to do so. God followed his own requirements of atonement for sin through sacrifice.

The Lord said to Cain, "What have you done? Listen! Your brother's blood cries out to me from the ground." Imagine the sound of all of the aborted babies' blood crying out to God from their graves!

When we sin or disconnect from God, He continues to care for us and wants the best for us. Even as we are yet sinners, He gave His Son for us to be reconciled to Him. There are consequences as Cain was cast out from the land and from the presence of God. So sad the consequences of anger, violence, and murder....

respond

How much do I know about technology and its dangers?

What can I do to protect myself and my loved ones from becoming addicted to the use of technology, pornography, and paths of self-destruction?

What can I do to learn more about the Knowledge of Good, i.e. Knowledge of God, to help me navigate the world outside the Garden of Eden?

If I would hear God calling, "Where are you?" in reference to my sins, where am I in my walk with the Lord, and how would I answer His question:

"Where are you?"

resolve

_____

_____

_____

_____

_____

_____

_____

_____

_____

_____

_____

_____

_____

Day 3

Genesis Chapters 5 & 6

HIGHLIGHTED TEXT:

- Genesis 5:24 Enoch walked with God 300 years (lived 365 years); then he was no more, because God took him away.
- Genesis 5:32 After Noah was 500 years old, he became the father of Shem, Ham and Japheth.
- Genesis 5:26-29 Lamech, Noah's father, spoke over his son Noah as he named him to become a comfort in the labor and painful toll of our hands caused by the ground the Lord has cursed.
- Genesis 6:5 The Lord saw how great man's wickedness on the earth had become and that every inclination of the thoughts of his heart was only evil all the time. 6:8 God's heart was filled with pain.
- Genesis 6:8 But Noah found favor in the eyes of the Lord.
- Genesis 6:18 God re-establishes his covenant with Noah as God plans that "everything on earth will perish."
- Genesis 6:22 says that Noah did EVERYTHING just as God commanded him.

reflect

Enoch was alive 65 years before he "walked with God." We are never too old (or too young!) to walk with God.

Noah was 500 years old when he built the ark. We know that his sons went on the ark with him when he answered the call of God to build the ark with no rain clouds in sight.

In God's mind, we are never too old to be called.

As Noah's father, Lamech, spoke over his son, Noah was to be a blessing of human toil within the land that was cursed. We parents need to be praying blessings over our children from conception and speak into their lives.

The Lord was grieved that he had made man on the earth, and his heart was filled with pain. God "saw that it was good" when he made man, but God has regrets as he watches his creations grow more evil by the days. As much joy as God had at our creation, He is now filled with pain (verse 6).

Our destiny turns on one man who found favor in the eyes of God. So must each of us be at least ONE person who finds favor with God, and we can change the world!

God is an all or nothing God. He wants our total obedience: all of us, not just partial obedience or loyalty to Him. When humanity turned so sinful that God wanted to destroy us all, ONE person (Noah!) was able to turn the tide of our destiny from total destruction to salvation. Through Noah's construction of an ark, according to God's very specific instructions, dimensions, and purpose, humanity was saved!

God is an EVERYTHING kind of God who wants EVERYTHING from us.

When Genesis 6:5 talks of the wickedness of the human heart, God wasn't just talking about Adam and Eve. He was talking about everybody. We start seeing an increase in violence. We see the darkness dispelled from the beginning starts to come back in. What God had created was being destroyed by every dark thing that people put in the world. Even in times of pandemic with COVID and quarantine at home, we saw chaos and death, like the deaths of George Floyd, Breonna Taylor, and the chaos in politics. We think that we have power and control to shape what God had already created. We think that we are not accepted, so we are going to find everything in our power to be accepted, but we're still not. We forgot that we are already accepted by God.

respond

When have I thought that I was being obedient to God? Have I obeyed Him to the fullest, or have I obeyed to the level of "minimal compliance"? When

I have said "yes" to the Lord, have I said "yes" to whatever still feels comfortable, safe, and risk-free? What do I need to do to become fully obedient to the Lord? Where am I holding back, and why?

resolve

_____

_____

_____

_____

_____

_____

_____

_____

_____

_____

_____

_____

_____

_____

_____

_____

_____

_____

_____

_____

_____

_____

Day 4

read

Genesis Chapter 7

HIGHLIGHTED TEXT:

- Genesis 7:4 "Seven days from now I will send rain on the earth for forty days and forty nights, and I will wipe from the face of the earth every living creature I have made."

- Genesis 7:12 And rain fell on the earth forty days and forty nights.

- Genesis 7:16 Then the Lord shut him in.

- Genesis 7:17 For forty days the flood kept coming on the earth, and as the waters increased they lifted the ark high above the earth.

- Genesis 7:24 The waters flooded the earth for a hundred and fifty days.

reflect

There is something significant in the waiting of the 40 days. Floods overflow. There is something significant about being in the overflow, of being submerged with God, just as Jesus spent 40 days in the wilderness being submerged with the Father. Maybe we can't just tip our toes in the water; maybe we have to be completely submerged. We need to submerge ourselves with God, to get deep with Him. Healing doesn't happen on the surface; it happens in the deep.

n Besides the waters receding, Noah had to wait until he, his family, and the animals could safely disembark. This is a lesson, not only in obedience to God, but in patience and waiting on God to fulfill His purposes for our lives. Not all miracles, healings, and salvations are immediate. Some of God's blessings take time and requires us to wait. Try waiting on anything for 150 days before proceeding to the next step in a plan, project, or process. Waiting on God is worth it, but we have to practice patience to be strong enough to receive the blessing when God is ready to deliver it (or us!)

Sometimes God closes the door and shuts us in, away from things that will harm us. He makes us wait until the coast is clear (literally for Noah!) Even when we don't understand why or how long we have to wait, God keeps the door closed for our own protection. Noah could have escaped, but he had nowhere to go but overboard without a place to land. It was best for him and his family to stay put for a while and wait on God. I sure wish that I would remember that the next time a door closes in my face.

I am sure that Noah and his family were ready to get out of the ark to walk on land again. They had to wait; to stay quarantined on a big boat to escape destruction. When they finally disembarked, Noah built an altar to the Lord.

respond

What is the longest that I have ever prayed for someone or something before I gave up and stopped praying?

What examples in my life give me hope in the waiting for miracles or blessings to come to someone?

How long am I willing to wait on God...for anything?

We usually ask, "How long, O God?"

Maybe God also waits on us and asks, "How long, O Child?"

What are events in my life where God has saved me from destruction?

When have I been so thankful to God that I have built an altar to Him in thanks and remembrance of what He has done for me?

resolve

_____

_____

_____

_____

_____

_____

_____

_____

_____

_____

_____

_____

Day 5

read

Genesis Chapter 8

HIGHLIGHTED TEXT:

- Genesis 8:1 "But God remembered Noah and all the wild animals and livestock that were with him in the ark, and he sent a wind over the earth, and the waters receded."

- Genesis 8:6 After forty days Noah opened a window he had made in the ark

- Genesis 8:20 "Then Noah built an altar to the Lord and, taking some of all the clean animals and clean birds, he sacrificed burnt offerings on it," and it says in verse 21 "the Lord smelled the pleasing aroma and said that he never again would curse the ground because of man, even though every inclination of his heart is evil from childhood."

reflect

God remembered Noah, and Noah remembered God. There are thoughts and feelings between the two, so as there are today between God and us. God loved the smell of a good grilled food intended especially for him. As he is breathed in the delicious aroma,

He felt endearing toward man, knowing at the same time that man's heart is inclined to evil from childhood. That evil is the sole independence that we crave, regardless of what God says or wants for us. From the time we are children, we fight our parents to do things on our own, to be on our own, to do what we want to do, regardless of the consequences that children cannot foresee. How loving is our God that knows we are sinners, yet continues to love when we show him appreciation and love back.

Even in pandemics and times of world turmoil, we remember verse 22: "As long as the earth endures, seedtime and harvest, cold and heat, summer and winter, day and night will never cease." There is still hope. The world has been in chaos for centuries, yet it continues, as does God's love for us.

All I need to meditate on today is that "God remembered." God remembers his people and his creation. Sometimes when I wonder if God has forgotten about me, or if I think that he really doesn't keep his promises, I think about Noah. Noah was waiting for the waters to recede for 150 days.

God remembers. God remembers His promises and His children. The entire Bible is the history of God's fulfillment of His promise to us.

Noah kept sending out a dove to see if there was dry land. The diligence and patience of being submerged with God is incredible. If Adam and Eve had just gone deeper with God, they would have remembered that they had so much. God had created the world in seven days and fulfilled their every desire. He could have answered their questions. God still wanted to multiply in the earth. He remembered that he created humans and the earth in His image, so He knew that the earth would grow again after the flood. Plants need water to grow. John talks about "if you drink this water, you'll never thirst again." But Adam and Eve did not talk to God about their thoughts and questions; they listened to the serpent instead and became confused about God's clear instructions.

---

respond

How often do I remember God?

How often do I remember promises that I have made in the presence of God and in the name of Jesus?

How often do I remember family, friends, and lost souls in my prayer times?

How often do I remember to thank God for all that He has done for us?

How far am I from God spiritually? Do I even know where I am?

---

resolve

_____

_____

_____

_____

_____

_____

_____

_____

_____

_____

_____

_____

_____

Day 6

read

Genesis Chapters 9 & 10

HIGHLIGHTED TEXT:

- Not only did God bless Noah and his sons, saying to them to be fruitful and multiply, God also said in Genesis 9:5 "And for your lifeblood I will surely demand an accounting. I will demand an accounting from every animal. And from each man, too, I will demand an accounting for the life of his fellow man."

- Genesis 9:11 God establishes his covenant with his words, "Never again will all life be cut off by the waters of a flood; never again will there be a flood to destroy the earth."

- Genesis 9:16 Whenever the rainbow appears in the clouds, I will see it and remember the everlasting covenant between God and all living creatures of every kind on the earth."

- Genesis 9:21 When he drank some of its wine, he became drunk and lay uncovered inside his tent.

reflect

God sees that we continue to cause destruction, to break covenants and to break with the will of God. However, God continues to want to redeem us, to give us a chance for us to be fruitful and multiply. Even if we don't remember, God remembers. God is not dependent on us to keep his covenant.

We see Noah slipping up in Chapter 9:21 when he became drunk and lay uncovered. This is an example of self-desire that always draws people away from God. Right after the rainbow, Noah gets drunk. He wasn't satisfied with drinking the fruit of the vine, but he drank in excess, more than what he needed. This also affected his sons and their actions that led to Cain being cursed. Actions that started with the father affected the sons. The examples we set for our children are keys to them being blessed or cursed. We continue to go back to our fleshly desires. We need to guard ourselves from what we do immediately after a rainbow experience.

Adam was given the honor of naming every living creature. However, man was not given total authority of creation, but he was made accountable for creation by God. God retains his authority over all of us, humans and animals, and requires, no, demands an accounting for the life of his fellow man.

This is an overwhelming charge, to account for the life of our fellow man. To me, this means that I am required to tell others about God if they don't know, and to do what I can for their lives. To love God and to serve the Lord and our fellow human beings. And with our supreme intelligence that tops the creations of God, we need to use our intelligence and our love to care for all animals and everything that works toward sustaining them. God holds us accountable for life.

This seems to be an even larger scope of responsibility; we are to consider how we are managing the earth and its resources. We are to consider gravely what we do to preserve life. That is a high order from the highest authority, the God who made us.

I used to think that the rainbow in the sky was a sign for me to remember the covenant, but verse 16 says that when God sees the rainbow appearing in the clouds, God will remember this "everlasting covenant between God and ALL living creatures of every kind on the earth."

Typically we may think about this covenant between God and man and all our descendants, but the Word states that this promise is made also to every living creature on earth. I don't own any pets, but I enjoy observing how other pet owners fawn over their dogs, cats, birds, horses, iguanas, and snakes. The relationship between the pet owner and the pet looks authentic to me, at least when I see my granddaughter's service dog, Bowser, stay by her side, count on her to be fed, and go on adventures with her in the park or wading in a creek bed. There is a co-dependent connection that rivals some human to human relationships. There must be a magnanimous connection between the creator and the animals he created.

If the Creator has promised not to destroy the entire earth with another flood, then I wonder why humans do so many things that are destroying our earth. Our actions directly affect our fellow creatures in this world. When I watch nature documentaries about species that are threatened by man's greediness, ignorance, or entertainment, I think that God has more confidence in nature than in man in preserving the world He made for us.

respond

How do I see myself in connection with all other creatures on Earth?

How do I see my relationship with God?

Do I feel all the authority that has been handed to me by my Creator and an expectation to spend eternity with God?

Or do I live with a feeling of impending doom because of my past mistakes and because of the reality of an eternal hell away from God?

resolve

_____

_____

_____

_____

_____

_____

_____

_____

_____

_____

_____

_____

_____

Day 7

read

Genesis Chapter 11

HIGHLIGHTED TEXT:

- Genesis 11:1 Now the whole world had one language and a common speech.

- Genesis 11:6-8 The Lord said, "If as one people speaking the same language they have begun to do this, then nothing they plan to do will be impossible for them. Come, let US go down and confuse their language so they will not understand each other." So the Lord scattered them from there over all the earth, and they stopped building the city.

reflect

The people wanted to build themselves a city with a tower that reaches to the heavens, so that we may MAKE A NAME FOR OURSELVES and not be scattered over the face of the whole earth.

Typically unity and collaboration are admirable characteristics of leadership and people working together for the same purpose. However, when that purpose has the intention of working in opposition with God and His purposes, unity and collaboration can become an evil force. In all cases, God is still in control and can stop whatever it is that humans can devise contrary to His will for our lives.

We talk way too much. We just "babble on." We overthink and get our thoughts away from God, so God put a stop to our group thinking of trying to be more powerful than God.

respond

Have I ever had a time when I have experienced unity of thought with others and realized that we worked together better and stronger than by working alone or in isolation?

What did I do to contribute to the end results?

Have I ever had a time when I was thinking the same thoughts as others, but then realized that we were all misguided and working against God's will for us?

What did I do to change our circumstances, and was I successful?

How did the others respond? What were the end results of my actions?

resolve

_____

_____

_____

_____

_____

_____

_____

_____

_____

_____

_____

_____

_____

Day 8

Genesis Chapter 12

HIGHLIGHTED TEXT:

- Genesis 12:1 The Lord had said to Abram, "Go from your country, your people and your father's household to the land I will show you.
- 12:1 The Lord had said to Abram, "Leave your country, your people, and your father's house and to the land I will show you."
- 12:2 "I will make you into a great nation
     And I will bless you;
     I will make your name great,
     And you will be a blessing.
     I will bless those who bless you,
     And whoever curses you I will curse;
     And all people on earth
     Will be blessed through you."

- Genesis 12:4 So Abram left, as the Lord had told him; and Lord with him. Abram was seventy-five years old when he set out from Haram....
- Genesis 12:7 The Lord appeared to Abram and said, "To your offspring I will give this land." So he built an altar there to the Lord, who had appeared to him.
- Genesis 12:8 From there he went on toward the hills east of Bethel and pitched his tent, with Bethel on the west and AI on the east. There he built an altar to the Lord and called on the name of the Lord. Then Abram set out and continued toward Negev.

- Genesis 12:10 Famine hits and Abram goes to Egypt for a while. He lies and says that his wife Sarai is his sister. Pharoah takes Sarai and treats Abram well, but the Lord inflicts serious illnesses on Pharoah and family. Pharoah says to Abram, "Take her and go!" Gen. 12:20

reflect

Everything in this world is temporary. In Luke, Peter left everything to follow Jesus. Are we willing to drop everything for God? Abram was called to be different, not called to fit in. When he is building a nation, he would have to be different, to be better, to be called out of normalcy. He had to be in a whole new mindset. Even today, we can't be stagnant; we have to build the kingdom that is bigger than where we are right now. God told Abram, "You are bigger than what you are right now."

The Lord tells Abram to Leave and Go! With His promise of blessing him, making his name great, and all people on earth blessed through him. So worth the leaving and going with promises like this from the Lord!!

God keeps Abram moving to fulfill the promise that God made to him, regardless of Abram's age. When Abram does stop, he takes the time to build an altar to the Lord, to mark the importance of God's Word to him, to pray and praise God, and to remember the incredible event that has just taken place.

For people who think that they are too old to hear from God, too old to start a new life or ministry or mission, we have Abram as an example setting out at the age of 75, leaving his former life behind him.

respond

What are some times or events in my life when God has asked me to move, to change, to take a step forward in my spiritual life?

How old was I?

How have I remembered or marked this important "milestone" so that I never forget?

If God told me to "go" today, am I willing to uproot all that I know and go?

resolve

_____

_____

_____

_____

_____

_____

_____

_____

_____

_____

_____

_____

Day 9

read

Genesis Chapter 13

HIGHLIGHTED TEXT:

* Genesis 13:2 Abram's wife makes him rich in livestock and in silver and gold.

* Genesis 13:3 Abram returns to his first altar to the Lord and called on the name of the Lord.

* Genesis 13:8 Abram splits the land with his brother Lot because their people were quarreling.

* Genesis 13:14 The Lord promises Abram all the land that he can see for him and his offspring forever. Abram moves again to live near the great trees of Mamre at Hebron, where he built an altar to the Lord.

reflect

Within God's promise to give Abram a legacy of innumerable children, God also provided Abram with a wife who gave him children, as well as riches in the forms of livestock, silver and gold. God fully fulfills promises with more than we could ever imagine, including the resources and support that we need to live in the promise. Subsequently, Abram returned to his first altar and called on the Lord. Obediently and without question,

Abram splits his land with his brother (giving Lot "a lot" to avoid family quarreling), AND Abram gives Lot the first pick of the property! Even so, God promises Abram all the land that he can see for him and his offspring, that is, enough land that more than supplies his needs for him and his offspring forever. That is a God-sized commitment that offers much and that is without end.

God was implementing ways to be Christ like by the example of giving. God didn't mean for us to keep all the resources to ourselves but to be a resource for other people. We knew that we would always be filled, that God would always supply our needs. Even when we have no more to give, God continues to give to us so that we can give to other people. Just like with the loaves and fish, there was an endless supply. God continued to supply. There is always a supplier and a demand, and God says that he will fulfill our needs. Abraham had the faith to give away all that land, and he knew that he would still be alright.

respond

Do I share my resources only when I have extra or don't feel the pinch of giving?

Do I feel the need to stay in control of my gifts (tithes, offerings)?

Am I satisfied to give away the best of what I have and be content with what is left?

Do I know that God will continue to bless me beyond measure?

In settling quarrels or conflicts, how easy is it for me to allow others to be in control?

Am I willing to sacrifice for the sake of peace so that everyone "wins", even if it costs me something?

resolve

Day 10

read

Genesis Chapter 14

HIGHLIGHTED TEXT:

- Genesis 14:11-12 Four kings seized all the goods of Sodom and Gomorrah and all their food; then they went away. They also carried off Abram's nephew Lot and his possessions, since he was living in Sodom.

- Genesis 14:14-16 When Abram heard that his relative had been taken captive, he called out the 318 trained men born in his household and went in pursuit as far as Dan. During the night, Abram (1) divided his men to attack them and (2) he routed them, (3) pursued them as far as Hobah, north of Damascus. (4) He recovered all the goods and brought back his relative Lot and his possessions, together with the women and the other people.

- Genesis 14:20 Abram tithes a tenth of everything.

reflect

Selfishness has become embedded in our culture. Abram rejected the selfish intent of the king, who was giving purely out of self. Abram continues to be an example of what the covenant of God is supposed to look like, that of people being in God's image and being created in His likeness.

Abram did everything he could to protect his family and possession. Strategically he used his men effectively and pursued the enemy until he recovered ALL the goods, Lot and all his people and possessions. Having recovered everything, Abram sets an example for us by tithing a tenth of everything he owns to the high priest Melchizedek, king of Salem, but Abram refuses to accept any gifts from the king of Sodom. Abram speaks of his oath of allegiance to God the Almighty and proclaims that no man (or king) will be able to say that he made Abram rich. Abram credits everything he is and owns to God.

Take somebody with you on your journey! You don't have to go it alone.

respond

There are times when we are forced with decisions about how we protect what is ours and from whom we receive gifts or favors. When have I had to make a decision that cost me something but was rooted in my loyalty and commitment to God and His commands?

Have I ever compromised my promise to God, intentionally or unintentionally, in my dealings with other people, in the business world, or other areas of my life?

resolve

Day 11

Genesis Chapter 15

HIGHLIGHTED TEXT:

THE GREAT PROMISE OF PROSPERITY!

- Genesis 15:1 God tells Abram not to be afraid, that He is Abram's shield and his very great reward. Immediately Abram asks God, "O Sovereign Lord, what can you give me since I remain childless and the one will inherit my estate is Eliezer of Damascus? You have given me no children; so a servant in my household will be my heir."
- Genesis 15:5 He took him outside and said, "Look up at the heavens and count the stars—if indeed you can count them." Then he said to him, "So shall your offspring be."

THE TERMS OF THE PROMISE

- Genesis 15:8 Abram asks God for a sign of his promise, so God has him make a sacrifice of a heifer, a goat, and a ram with a dove and a pigeon. Then in a deep sleep, the Lord tells Abram that it's not going to be all that easy to receive the blessing.
- Genesis 15:13 "Know for certain that your descendants will be strangers in a country not their own, and they will be enslaved and mistreated for 400 years....You, however, will go to your fathers in peace and be buried at a good old age...." And God continues mapping out his plan for Abram and his people. Then God sets His own fire for the sacrifice after the sun had set and darkness had fallen...a smoking firepot with a blazing torch appeared and passed between the pieces.

reflect

God takes Abram outside and tells him to look up and count the stars – if indeed he can count them. God intended for Abram to have many offspring, as he intends many blessings for us. When God tells us that He will bless us, why do we have to jump right in and state what we think we need? He already knows... and so much more.

Nothing is impossible with God. Not only does he set the terms of His promises and covenant, He lights his own fire for the sacrifice, interestingly, not from the heat of the burning midday sun, but after the sun had set and darkness had fallen. God sets the covenant on fire and makes it happen! Quite a spectacle of the impossible becoming possible on God's terms. God acts in these ways so that there is no mistaking who has the power and who gets the glory.

God was thinking beyond the box that Abram was in and what he could see. God wanted Abram to fix his eyes on Him, and beyond, not on Abram himself. That's why he had him look at the stars. Just as a parent wants a child to have eye contact, God was saying to Abram, "Look at me when I'm talking to you (into the heavens and at the stars)." God tells Abram, "I'm here to set you up for prosperity, but you need to trust me so I can usher you into the plan where I want you to go."

respond

Abram asked God, "What can you give me...?"

Do I do the same in my prayer life, asking what God can give me and do for me rather than thanking Him for what He has already provided and for His promise to be faithful to me and my family always?

resolve

_____

_____

_____

_____

_____

_____

_____

Day 12

read

Genesis Chapter 16

HIGHLIGHTED TEXT:

WAIT FOR GOD'S PROMISE TO UNFOLD

- Genesis 16:2 Sarai, Abram's wife, was barren and doesn't wait for God's promise, as she tells her husband Abram," Go, sleep with my maidservant; perhaps I can build a family through her." And Abram agrees....just like the Garden of Eden. The woman wants to play God and the man follows her invitation to join her, followed by misguided blame as she tells Abram he is responsible for the "wrong I am suffering." Abram puts the decision back into Sarai's hands; she mistreats Hagar, so Hagar flees.

- Genesis 16:7 Hagar pursued by the angel of the Lord, "Hagar, servant of Sarai, where have you come from, and where are you going?" She responds that she is running away from her mistress, but the angel sends her back: "Go back to your mistress and submit to her." She is being sent back to the place where she was mistreated, but Hagar gets the same promise as Abram from God: "I will so increase your descendants that they will be too numerous to count."

- Genesis 16: 13 Hagar is to name her child Ismael (God hears) and she names the Lord who spoke to her, "You are the God who sees me." And the well was named Beer Lahai Roi meaning "well of the Living One who sees me." Hagar has to submit and return....even with a "wild donkey of a child" who will live in hostility with all his brothers.

- Genesis 16:15 Hagar bore Abram a son, and Abram gave him the name Ishmael....even though the father named the children, Abram used the name given to Hagar by the angel.

reflect

At first Sarai was mad at Hagar, but Sarai was the one who couldn't wait on the promise that God had for her and her husband. She pushed family on Abram and mistreated Hagar. Sarai was fulfilling her own needs, but then hated the woman that she put in place to do so.

Hagar gets blessed from Sarai's ignorance. As Abram slept with Hagar, Sarai missed her waiting period. Actually, both Sarai and Hagar missed their waiting period for God to bless them as Hagar ran away from her mistress, Sarai, when the angel of the Lord pursued her to return (to repent or turn back). When Hagar returned, she received her blessing from God. God had bigger blessings in mind for Abram, Sarai, and Hagar, but they took action instead of waiting on God.

When the Hagar's "donkey of a child" showed hostility, he had just taken on the characteristics that the parents had created in the household. It was easy to place blame on something or someone who is blameless. Who really was the stubborn, disobedient donkey in the story? Was it just the child, or all three: Abram, Sarai, and Hagar?

This is a testimony that God does see us, even when we jump ahead of God's promises or run from our problems. When we use our gift of free will unwisely, God may have us step backward to the point of His promise to regroup so that He can bless us, even with consequences, such as living with "a wild donkey of a child."

---

respond

When have I jumped ahead of God and tried to rush the fulfillment of his purpose for me?

Have I ever acted like a "wild donkey of a child" and caused hostility with my brothers and sisters?

When have I misplaced blame on something or someone who was blameless?

How do I know that I am in God's perfect will for me?

If I would hear God calling, "Where are you?" in reference to my sins, where am I in my walk with the Lord, and how would I answer His question:

"Where are you?"

---

resolve

_____

_____

_____

_____

_____

_____

_____

_____

_____

_____

_____

_____

_____

Day 13

Genesis Chapter 17

HIGHLIGHTED TEXT:

SIGNIFICANT CHANGE IN IDENTITY – WHO HAS GOD CALLED YOU TO BE?

- Genesis 17:1 God tells Abram, "I am God Almighty; walk before me faithfully and be blameless. I will confirm my covenant between me and you and will greatly increase your numbers."
- Genesis 17:5 Abram's name changed to Abraham... significant event! Everlasting covenant, everlasting possession of land to him and his descendants.

AGREEMENT TO THE TERMS OF THE PROSPERITY PROMISE

- Genesis 17:9 Abraham must keep God's covenant through circumcision as a sign...every person offspring or foreigner in the household must be circumcised... Jews and "Gentiles" Uncircumcised are to be "cut off" from his people...or circumcised from his people.
- Genesis 17:15 Sarai becomes Sarah...kings of peoples will come from her.
- Genesis 17:17 Abraham laughs...a joke at his age of 100 to have a son...God names the child "he laughs" – Isaac (no joke!)
- Genesis 17:23 ON THAT VERY DAY, Abraham had every male circumcised. Ishmael was 13, Abraham 99.
- named the children, Abram used the name given to Hagar by the angel.

reflect

Abraham (and other Biblical leaders) built altars to God to mark significant events, life defining moments. Additionally, significant moments were and still are marked by meaningful names at birth. God marked significant moments, life defining moments, by renaming people, as Abram became Abraham and Sarai became Sarah. Parents give great attention to the names of their children, and as adults, we add titles to our names to denote milestones or to give special recognition: Dr., Mrs. Rev., Your Honor, Sir, etc. Sometimes adults change their childhood nicknames back to their God-given birth names. They have also renamed themselves because of a new stage in their lives. Just as God the Creator spoke His Word into being, we speak meaning into our lives through names that we call ourselves and others. Names frame our identities.

It is significant that God called Abram to the place where he was supposed to go. God knows our names. Scripture says "Before I was born the Lord called me; from my mother's womb he has spoken my name." (Isaiah 49:1) "For you created my inmost being; you knit me together in my mother's womb." (Psalm 139:13) God calls us by name, and our names make us accountable. They come with nobility, family, and purpose.

They identify to whom we belong. Abram and Sarai were renamed from out of their earthly domain and into the covenant with God. He was directing their path.

respond

When have I undergone a change in my identity by a new nickname, new name, or new title?

How did that affect my thoughts and actions?

If God were to rename me today, what kind of name would it be and how would it describe the essence of my being?

resolve

_____

_____

_____

Day 14

read

Genesis Chapters 9 & 10

HIGHLIGHTED TEXT:

THE IMPORTANCE OF HOSPITALITY AND RELATIONSHIPS

- Genesis 18:2 Three visitors come to Abraham and he HURRIES to meet them and bows low to the ground. 18:7 Abraham RUNS to the herd to select a choice, tender calf and gave it to his servant, who HURRIED to prepare it.

- Genesis 18:12 Sarah laughs at the news of a child when she is beyond childbearing years. (For God, age is not an issue.) Then she lies about laughing to the Lord.

GOD LISTENS AND GOD SAVES

- Genesis 18:24 What if Abraham can find 50 righteous people in Sodom?

- Genesis 18:28 45 righteous people?

- Genesis 18:29 40 righteous people?

- Genesis 18:30 30 righteous people?

- Genesis 18:31 20 righteous people?

- Genesis 18:32 10 righteous people? God answers, "For the sake of ten, I will not destroy it."

reflect

Having to search for righteous people in Sodom emphasized how Abraham had to think about what is righteousness and who was righteous.

Hospitality is the main characteristic of being a Christian. Brothers and sisters in Christ should not feel out of place. We share the same heart in the same body of Christ. "

Two are better than one,
because they have a good return for their labor:
If either of them falls down,
one can help the other up.
But pity anyone who falls
and has no one to help them up.
Also, if two lie down together, they will keep warm.
But how can one keep warm alone?
Though one may be overpowered,
two can defend themselves.
A cord of three strands is not quickly broken.

Ecclesiastes 4:9-12

We may think of the Old Testament as books of rules, laws, and traditions, but there is also a strong theme of relationships and hospitality. Visitors, even perfect strangers, were welcomed into the home with food and comfort in a timely manner, as seen in this example of Abraham.

All things are possible with God, even childbirth for an old woman like Sarah. This may have seemed preposterous, and even worthy of a good laugh, but when confronted by God, Sarah lies about laughing.

God was patient with Abraham in trying to save Sodom. Abraham was questioning God's plan, but God allowed Abraham to work through his thought process regarding the level of righteousness in his community. As much as Abraham tried, he could not find 50, or even 10, people who were righteous. The city of Sodom was in such decline that unrighteousness was the norm for everyone.

respond

How has hospitality changed for us today?

How do I respond when strangers approach me or my home?

Why did Sarah lie to God about laughing?

If God asked me to search for 50 righteousness people, would I be included in the 50?

Would I be able to find 50, or 10, who could say that they are righteous in the eyes of God?

Do I live in a community surrounded by righteous people?

Am I in a community of at least 50 righteous people, or am I isolated in my community of one or with just my family?

How important is community to maintain a life of righteousness? Am I influenced by them or do I influence them to live a life of righteous?

How does my city/state/country compare to Sodom? How evil does one have to be for God to consider destroying it?

Define "righteousness." What does it look like? What does it feel like?

resolve

Day 15

Genesis Chapter 19

HIGHLIGHTED TEXT:

- Genesis 19:1 Two angels come to Lot's house in Sodom, and Lot's hospitality moves him to protect them. "Don't do anything to these men, for they have come under the protection of my roof." The angels strike the crowd with blindness. The angels asked Lot to get the rest of his family. When he told his sons-in-law, they thought he was joking. 19:14

- Genesis 19:16 When Lot hesitated, the angels grabbed his hand and the hands of his wife and two daughters and led them safely out of the city, for the Lord was merciful. Genesis 19:19 Lot can't flee to the mountains and asks for a nearby town. God consents.

- Genesis 19:26 Lot's wife looked back and became a pillar of salt. Genesis 19:30 Lot and family flee to the mountains out of Zoar because they did not feel safe. God said that he would protect the town with them living there. NOW he complies to God's first instruction to flee to the mountains, where they lived in a cave, where both daughters lay with their father Lot and had children: Moab and Ben Ammi.

reflect

*S*ometimes we change our destiny by our requests to God. Sometimes we are paralyzed by inaction and a lack of faith. The angels tried to save Lot's sons-in-law, and they thought God's provision was a joke. Lot hesitated, and the angels had to grab his hand to get him to move...to save himself and his family! Even when Lot knew that he was supposed to flee to the mountains, he asked God for a Plan B, a nearby town instead, to which God agrees. Even when we ask to amend God's plan, God allows our free will and requests to change His original plan for us. By the time Lot's wife looked back, she was out of chances to move forward. She was permanently "paralyzed" in salt. There is danger in looking back to your former life.

*L*ot struggled to go where God directed him, perhaps because Lot had become too comfortable. He had moved from place to place for years, so he was happy to just settle finally in a nearby town rather than the mountains. God shifts us out of our places of comfort because he wants to grow us and bless us. When we become comfortable, we may be missing what God has planned for us. We miss opportunities to grow with God. He wanted to take Lot to newer and higher heights in the mountains, but Lot settled for his own Plan B, which God allowed out of the free will that he gave to humankind.

Just as Sarai, Abram, and Hagar took action instead of waiting for God to guide them, Lot's daughters took action when God did not order it. They slept with their father, Lot, and had children. The daughters didn't know how long they would be living in the cave of Zoar. Perhaps God would have provided for their family line in a way that was not incestuous. Perhaps from growing up in Sodom, the daughters were affected by the unrighteous environment and did not trust God to guide them from the darkness of the cave into a different life.

respond

Have I ever felt moved to follow God's plan for my future, but then asked for an easier, safer plan because of fear or inconvenience?

What do I need to do to go fearlessly ahead with God without hesitation, inaction, or a lack of faith?

resolve

Day 16

read

Genesis Chapter 20

HIGHLIGHTED TEXT:

ACTING WITH A CLEAR CONSCIENCE

- Genesis 20 NOW Abraham MOVED ON from there, but he lied about his wife Sarah in the new region of the Negev.
- Genesis 20:6 When God appeared to Abimelech in a dream, God told him that he acted with a clear conscience and kept him from sinning. God asked for Sarah to be returned to Abraham, whom God said is a prophet.
- Genesis 20:14 Abimelech offers restitution of sheep and cattle when he returned Sarah to him, and he also offered his land to live wherever Abraham liked. Abimelech vindicated Sarah, and Abraham prayed to God, and God healed Abimelech, his wife and slave girls so they could have children again (for God had closed their wombs because of Sarah).

reflect

Abraham did not have enough faith to tell the truth about Sarah being his wife. After all that he had experienced having faith in God, he chose an easier route, as did Sarah, who kept silent and went along with the lie.

When we act with clear consciences, we can trust that God will help us to keep us from sinning if we listen to him. Sometimes we cause problems unintentionally, but God lets us know if we stay close to Him.

Chapter 20 is an example of the ripple effect of lies and sin. It is an example of restitution and restoration. It is also an example of the ripple effect of forgiveness, restitution, and intercessory prayer. How one person acts really does matter to God and to other people.

respond

When have I not been entirely up front with information and possibly lied to someone to protect me, my family, or my pride?

Do I need to make restitution for anyone for whom I have offended?

resolve

_____

_____

_____

_____

_____

_____

_____

_____

_____

_____

_____

_____

Day 17

read

Genesis Chapter 21

HIGHLIGHTED TEXT:

GOD HEARS AND BLESSES

- Genesis 21:1 God's timing is perfect, and God makes good on his promise with a baby for Abraham and Sarah in their old age. Abraham was 100 years old when Isaac was born.
- Genesis 21 Sarah vs. Hagar -- God heard Sarah's laughter and Hagar's sobbing, and He answered both of them. God blesses all of Abraham's offspring, both from Sarah and from Hagar.
- Genesis 21:33 Abraham plants a tamarisk tree as he called upon the Lord.

reflect

 It's never too late when God wants to move in our lives.

Instead of building an altar of stones, Abraham plants a tree as he calls upon the Lord. God proves that He makes good on His promises. We need to make sure that we know all of God's promises in the Bible to increase our faith that He will fulfill them all.

This is about relationships. This shows how much God loves us. We are in such a hurry to get to the promises before we go through the process that God wants for us. We can see God in our laughter and in our tears in any situation.

respond

Is there anything that I have not done in the name of the Lord because I thought that I was the wrong age (too young or too old)?

Do I have a relationship with God that is fruitful enough that I could build an altar or plant a tree in response to His faithfulness in my life?

resolve

_____

_____

_____

_____

_____

_____

_____

_____

_____

_____

_____

_____

Day 18

Genesis Chapter 22

HIGHLIGHTED TEXT:

THE GREAT PROPHETIC SACRIFICE

- Genesis 22 God calls to Abraham, and three times, Abraham responds, "Here I am!" God asked for a sacrifice of obedience from Abraham first, and on the THIRD DAY, Abraham built the altar with his son Isaac.
- Genesis 22:8 Abraham trusted that God would provide the lamb for the offering.
- Genesis 22:12 God spares Isaac because Abraham did not withhold his son, as God says, "your son, your only son." Three times God says, "your son, your only son" in verses 2, 12, and 15. Three times Abraham says, "I am here."
- Genesis 22: 17 God restates his promise to Abraham of offspring of all nations on earth...

Abraham has to trust that God is going to provide, even though he doesn't see the evidence of it coming. This is a precursor to faith. Just because we don't see the evidence doesn't mean that God isn't

reflect

going to provide for us. God provided the lamb. Timing is so important. Our timing is not always the best, but God's timing is perfect: it is about the advancement of His Kingdom, faith in God and fear of God.

n There is a parallel between Abraham asking his servants to wait while he goes to worship and Jesus asking his disciples to wait with him while he prayed in the garden. Verse 6 Abraham carries the wood for the burnt offering of his firstborn son; Jesus carried his own wood (the cross) before his crucifixion.

respond

If I set aside time to listen to God and to say to Him, "Here I am!" what would God say to me?

Is there a parallel between Abraham, Jesus, and Me in that I need to spend time alone with God?

Is there a parallel between Abraham and Jesus carrying a heavy load of wood and my calling from God to carry some heavy burden as a sacrifice to Him and a fulfillment of His promise for me?

resolve

_____

_____

_____

_____

_____

_____

_____

_____

_____

_____

_____

_____

_____

Day 19

Genesis Chapter 22

HIGHLIGHTED TEXT:

WHERE IS YOUR SPECIAL GOD PLACE?

- Genesis 23:9 Abraham offers full price for the burial site for Sarah, but Ephron the Hittite gives Abraham the field and cave in it free of charge. Abraham insists on paying for it, so they agreed to the terms and price. This property was near his special place of Mambre (where Abraham heard from God in Genesis 18:1)

reflect

"Location! Location! Location!" These are the three most important factors in choosing real estate in today's world. In Abraham's time, it was important to him that he set aside a proper burial site for his wife, Sarah, near his special place of Mambre.

We always have a place in God. For me, I would go outside feeling closer to God. God gives us a final place to go where we pass. God is Home.

respond

What special places do we have that remind us of God's blessings, grace, mercy, or provisions?

The altar where you gave your heart to the Lord?

The place where you prayed when God granted you a miracle?

Was it the operating room?

The doctor's office? A room in your home? A place in nature?

resolve

_____

_____

_____

_____

_____

_____

_____

_____

_____

_____

_____

_____

Day 20

read

Genesis Chapter 24

HIGHLIGHTED TEXT:

GOD IS ALWAYS AHEAD OF US

- Genesis 24:1 The Lord had blessed Abraham in every way.

- Genesis 24:12 Abraham's servant prayed to God for the day's success, and thereby for kindness to his master, Abraham.

- Genesis 24:15 Before he had finished praying, Rebekah appears with her water jar.

- Genesis 24 The hospitality theme runs strongly through the actions of Rebekah as she waters the camels. Not only does Rebekah quickly take care of the watering of the animals, she also offers straw, fodder, and a room for the night. (verse 25)

- Genesis 24:34-49 The servant gives his testimony and credits God "who led me on the right road" to get the granddaughter of his master's brother for his son.

- Genesis 24:52 With no hesitation after hearing the servant's testimony, Laban and Bethuel confirm that "this is from the Lord; we can say nothing to you one way or another." And Rebekah is given to the servant to take back for Abraham's son.

- Genesis 24:55 Rebekah's family tries to detain her from going immediately, but she says, "I will go" with no hesitation.

reflect

Even Abraham's servant was praying for his master's success. God is always seven steps ahead of us. Praying for the day's success means that we know that God has already ordained our day. Rebekah was so willing to say yes. She had so much faith that God was guiding her. God wants us to secure our faith in Him. He is always with us and ahead of us.

God is answering our prayer requests before we even finish asking Him for them. (No time wasted!)

Immediate obedience to God: this is the goal to which we must all strive. (No time wasted!)

respond

Do I feel like God has blessed me in every way?

If not, how can I set myself up to receive blessings?

Let me count my blessings so far and trust that God wants to bless me in every way.

resolve

Day 21

read

Genesis Chapters 25 & 26

HIGHLIGHTED TEXT:

GOD'S DOUBLE BLESSINGS

- Genesis 25:9 Abraham buried near Mamre, where God had appeared to him.
- Genesis 25:19 twin brothers Jacob and Esau...a double blessing! God doubly blessed Rebekah, who had been barren, and now was to give birth to two sons.
- Genesis 25:33 Esau was a sellout for food! Hungry, he sold his birthright to Jacob for bread and lentil stew

LIKE FATHER LIKE SON

- Genesis 26:4 God makes the same promise to Isaac as he did to Abraham. "I will make your descendants as numerous as the stars in the sky and will give them all these lands, and through your offspring all nations on earth will be blessed, because Abraham obeyed me and kept my requirements, my commands, my decrees and my laws."
- Genesis 26:7 Isaac lies about his wife (saying she is his sister) just as Abraham did of Sarah.
- Genesis 26:24 God appears to Isaac and repeats his promise of prosperity.
- Genesis 26:28 "We saw clearly that the Lord was with you."

reflect

We watch as the family line of Abraham unfolds, as God promised him. God promised Abraham many generations, but He did not promise that the family would be free from conflict. As important as the family legacy was to Abraham, soon after we read of his death, we read of his grandsons' struggle over their birthrights.

Isn't that what we all want....to be so close to the Lord that others also see "clearly that the Lord was with you"?

People still have flaws. Physical needs get in the way of our spiritual needs. Esau fell behind. His future and blessings could have been better, but he did not know how Jacob was going to deceive him. From fear, jealousy, selfishness, or whatever reason, Isaac put his wife and himself in jeopardy by lying about her status. Abraham told the same lie, apparently passing on his example and sin to his son. Children inherit parents' blessings as well as their sins and patterns of misbehaviors, unless the cycle is broken by repentance and reparation.

God is still God with the same blessing, even when people fail.

respond

How often do we allow our carnal, physical desires come before our desire to serve God?

What family conflicts do I experience that could be better?

Am I going to let desire keep me from doing what I need to do for God?

Do I just take up "space" instead of taking my "place" with God?

Have I ever been in a situation where I felt that lying was necessary for my survival?

Have I ever told lies about my spouse or relative to make my life easier or navigate for favor?

What blessings of mine from God would I want passed on to my children?

What patterns of misbehavior or sin would I want to break so that my children won't continue the cycle?

resolve

Day 22

read

Genesis Chapter 27

HIGHLIGHTED TEXT:

TURNING THE CULTURE UPSIDE DOWN

- Genesis 27:26 Abraham seals his blessing with a kiss for Isaac after Isaac sells himself to his father as his brother Esau. He "steals" Esau's blessing.
- Genesis 27:42 Esau plans to kill his brother Isaac, and he is described as having "fury".
- Genesis 28:1 Isaac calls for Jacob and blesses him. (vs. 3) "May God Almighty bless you and make you fruitful and increase your numbers until you become a community of peoples. May he give you and your descendants the blessing given to Abraham." Isaac passes on the legacy of Abraham's prosperity promise.

reflect

Anger is a dangerous human emotion that can cause us to say and do things that we will regret. Although anger is a natural response and understandable, we can control our anger through focus on God and the understanding that everyone sins, everyone fails, and everyone disappoints. Even righteous anger should not cause us to sin or to harm others. Thankfully,

Esau did not kill his brother, and the two eventually came to a point of forgiveness and peace.

Esau was so hungry to feed his own body that he sold his own birthright, even when he knew that his brother had his eye on it. Sometimes we set ourselves up and lose our promised land because of our selfishness and vulnerability for our blessings to be stolen.

Esau served others. Hospitality was a priority in their culture. Jacob looked for a place of power, but Esau continued to serve his mother and father. He was a better servant than Jacob.

In both cases, God continued to bless both Jacob and Esau, thus fulfilling His promises to their father.

respond

Have I ever been so angry or furious that I wanted to kill or hurt someone?

What caused me to feel that way, and what can I do to change my feelings or actions?

How do I trust God enough to know that I will still be blessed, regardless of unjust actions by another?

How do I manage my eating habits?

Do I get so hungry that I make poor decisions?

Do I compromise my health and future because I rush to satisfy my immediate needs or wants? How can I train myself to stay focused on what's best for my life, even in times of weakness?

resolve

_____

_____

_____

_____

_____

_____

_____

_____

_____

_____

_____

_____

_____

Day 23

read

Genesis Chapter 28

HIGHLIGHTED TEXT:

- Genesis 28:8 Esau marries Canaanite women to spite his father Isaac.
- Genesis 28: 10ff Jacob receives God's prosperity promise in a dream.

reflect

Children are always going to do things to spite their parents. Jacob really didn't deserve the promise, but he received it from God. Whether or not we are faithful to God, God remains faithful to us in His promises and provisions for us.

God communicates in dreams. The Holy Spirit does not rest in His communications. God speaks to us in our unconscious minds through dreams, where our minds our uncluttered and open to receiving a Word from the Lord. It may be the most intimate time to speak to us.

n Every parent wants the best for their child and hopes that their child marries someone with similar family values, morals, and spiritual compatibility. When parents set parameters and guidelines to ensure that their children will make good decisions, the children do not always comply, and sometimes defy. The best that we parents can do is to set expectations clearly, guide lovingly, and trust God for the rest. God will provide and will bless those who trust in Him.

---

respond

What issue in my family has caused parent/child division or discontent?

What prompted the conflict, and what could possibly resolve it?

Why is it important for children to make their own decisions as adults?

How does the Holy Spirit communicate with me?

Through dreams? Through Scripture?

What can I do to help the Lord to communicate with me more often or more clearly?

Am I open to hear what God wants to tell me?

resolve

_____

_____

_____

_____

_____

_____

_____

_____

_____

_____

_____

Day 24

read

Genesis Chapters 29 & 30

HIGHLIGHTED TEXT:

TRUE LOVE WAITS

- Genesis 29:20 True love waits. "Jacob served seven years to get Rachel, but they only seemed like a few days to him because of his love for her."
- Genesis 29:23 Walking in the father's footsteps... Jacob deceived his father for Esau's birthright; now Laban deceives Jacob and he lay with Leah instead of Rachel, but he worked another seven years to get Rachel.
- Genesis 29:31-35 Leah had three sons to get her husband to love her, but the jealousy between Rachel and Leah continued.
- Genesis 30 Jacob increases his flock by choosing the strongest sheep of the flock. He manipulates nature with what he feeds them and what he puts into their water.

reflect

There is God's will, and then there is human free will. In the case of Jacob, God wanted to extend the family line through Jacob, but it wasn't as easy as Jacob may have first thought. He had to work doubly hard, and actually ended up with two wives in the process. We could say that Jacob had double the chances to have children, but it was double the years of labor for him to marry both Leah and Rachel.

Leah also tried to get her husband to love her by birthing three children, but she also had to endure the jealousy of Rachel.

Jacob ended up with the best of Laban's flock of sheep, but he had to go to great lengths to feed and water the sheep to win them from Laban. As God continues to provide for His people, His provision does not always come at no cost on the part of His people.

This is full circle, showing what it is to "wait on the Lord." We can't haphazardly place ourselves and our purpose. We have to go along with God's promise. Some things need to be earned before they can be deserved. Jacob had the motivation and courage to cultivate his patience, obedience, hard work, and moral ethics. God teaches us ethics, morals, values, patience, etc. The seven years waiting for Rachel showed how Jacob was willing to work and to wait for what he thought was a part of his purpose. Jacob was then prepared to lead in his purpose with Rachel.

respond

As I pray for God's will in my life and walk the path that He intended for me, how much effort do I invest in bringing His promises to fulfillment?

Am I waiting for His gifts to be handed to me immediately and without work on my part?

Or am I willing to wait and to work hard, even as long as seven plus seven more years, to reap the rewards that He has for me?

resolve

_____

_____

_____

_____

Day 25

read

Genesis Chapter 31

HIGHLIGHTED TEXT:

CAN YOU GO HOME AGAIN?

- Genesis 31 God appears to Jacob in a dream, and Jacob answers, "Here I am." God tells him to go back to his native land.
- Genesis 31:24 God came to Laban the Aramean in a dream and told him not to say anything good or bad to Jacob.
- Genesis 31:35 Rachel uses her monthly period as an excuse, which is a lie: "Don't be angry, my lord, that I cannot stand up in your presence; I'm having my period."
- Genesis 31:49 "This heap is a witness between you and me today...May the Lord keep watch between you and me when we are away from each other." (Jacob and Laban)

reflect

We are not too far gone to come back to where God had us originally. Most of the time, when we come back, we are much better for it. Obedience to God shows how much you love Him. Obedience is a direct line to discipline. It is harder to stay disciplined if we don't stay obedient to God. God always has a plan and a place for us, even when friends or family may exclude us or make us feel that we are outcasts. God always has a plan and has a place for us. He already created our plan for us, so there's nothing to do but to be confident in where He has placed us.

As with Abraham answering God's call with, "Here I am," so does Jacob, Abraham's son. With Abraham, God was sending him somewhere new. In Jacob's case, God was sending back to his native land. Sometimes God doesn't send us to new places, but back home.

Sometimes we use excuses for not being obedient or compliant to commands. (And did you smile when you read that women used their monthly menses as an excuse? Still the oldest trick in "the book"!)

Family ties are strong, even when in-laws don't always get along. When we are together or far apart, it is right to ask for the Lord's blessing on family.

respond

Have I ever been guided "back home" again for a particular purpose?

How did I feel when I returned to a place where I had lived or worked?

Did it feel the same, and what was different?

How can God re-purpose us when we return to a familiar place?

Thinking of family members and in-laws who have joined my family through marriage, how can I pray for each one of them to make us all stronger in the faith and closer as family?

resolve

_____

_____

_____

_____

_____

_____

_____

_____

_____

_____

_____

_____

_____

Day 26

read

Genesis Chapters 32 &3

HIGHLIGHTED TEXT:

SPIRITUAL (AND PHYSICAL) WARFARE - WRESTLING WITH GOD

- Genesis 32:28 Jacob wrestles with God (angel) and develops a limp in his hip.
- Genesis 33:11 Esau's legacy restored as Jacob gives back.

reflect

Jacob was preparing to meet Esau and didn't know whether Esau would be out for vengeance or peace, so Jacob prayed and planned to make their meeting go well. In spite of his plans, Jacob was afraid. Instead of being confronted with Esau's army, Jacob was confronted with one man who jumped him and wrestled with him until daybreak. Getting off with his life and a lifelong limp, Jacob made peace with his brother and was able to give back to Esau much of what had been taken from his legacy.

Jacob lived with a lifelong limp and a lifelong regret toward his brother. Jacob suffered the consequence of his former life. His limp was a tangible way of remembering the night he wrestled for his life, and the limp is a memory trigger.

We all carry something with us, some disability or defect or situation that is a struggle. As followers of God and Jesus, we are all going to have some cross to bear, something that we struggle with, but in God we are not broken. We are spiritually fixed and placed by God.

We wrestle with our Creator, someone who is much, much bigger and stronger than we are. If we are created in the image of God, are we not then actually wresting with ourselves, with who we are and what our placement is to be? Because God wants to move us out of where we are, sometimes He has to wrestle with us to get us to change. He is trying to take us out of ourselves. That God even allowed Jacob to wrestle, or for us to wrestle with Him, He is preparing us for placement in His purpose.

Because God wants to move us out of the place where we are, we have to wrestle with who we are. God has to stretch us. He can't put us in a place of promise if we stay the way we are. It's like later in the Bible when it talks about putting new wine into old wine skins. We can't be where we used to be when God is trying to take us to another place. God allowed Jacob to wrestle with Him and with himself, so that by the time they were finished wrestling, God would be able to place Jacob where he needed to be.

respond

When has there been a life-changing time when I have wrestled with God and/or with another person?

What was the outcome?

Was I able to move forward with restitution and new purpose, much like Jacob with Esau?

f I am in the middle of a conflict with someone or with God, do I have a plan to end it in peace?

What may I have to sacrifice to do so?

resolve

_____

_____

_____

_____

Day 27

read

Genesis Chapter 34

HIGHLIGHTED TEXT:

REVENGE SEEMS HONORABLE BUT IS NOT REWARDED

- Genesis 34:1 The brothers Simeon and Levi get revenge for their sister Dinah's rape by deceiving them, getting all the men circumcised and then killing every male in the city and looting and plundering, taking all their wealth, women and children, and everything in their houses

reflect

Sometimes we try to take the place of God. We can't take control from God, even when it comes to people we want to protect. We have to remember that God is our Defender. God fights our battles. Sometimes we try to take the place of God, but we are human; we are flawed. When we take control, we take relationship out of the equation. We need to let God in our heart and to let God stay in control of our lives. We can never solve problems entirely by ourselves, because we are not God.

Sin affects not only the individual, but all those around the sinner. It is contagious and its devastating effects spread like wildfire. Justice and vengeance is God's, not ours. No matter how affected and offended we are by heinous crimes, we must not become sinners ourselves in our responses.

respond

What has been done to me or to one of my loved ones that causes me to want revenge, justice, or payback?

What am I called to do as a Christian to respond to my friend's or loved one's transgressor(s)?

resolve

_____

_____

_____

_____

_____

_____

_____

_____

_____

_____

_____

_____

Day 28

read

Genesis Chapter 35

HIGHLIGHTED TEXT:

BUILD AN ALTAR

- Genesis 35:10 Name change from Jacob to Israel with the repeated prosperity promise of Abraham. Jacob sets up a stone pillar to mark this momentous event (verse 14) where God had spoken to him.
- Genesis 35:18 As Rachel dies in childbirth, she names her son Ben-Oni (son of my trouble) but Isaac renames him Benjamin (son of my right hand). Genesis 35:27 Jacob came home to his father Isaac in Mamre and died there, surviving his sons Esau and Jacob, who buried him.

reflect

A name change signals a change in his parents' vision for him. This impacts the baby's destiny. How we are named, and how we frame people, and how we verbalize life-defining moments impacts how we see ourselves and our world.

150

God always has a vision for us, even if we don't see it. He always has a plan and a purpose for us. God has already planned our name. God even knew what our new name was going to be from the beginning.

respond

What are names that have been given to me, either by my parents or by other people?

How do birth names, family names, nicknames, and titles impact how I see myself and the world around me?

If I wanted to reframe my view of myself or my world, what name(s) would I give myself?

If God were to name me today, what would it be?

How would he describe me and my future by His name for me?

resolve

_____

_____

_____

_____

_____

_____

_____

_____

_____

_____

_____

_____

Day 29

read

Genesis Chapters 36 & 37

HIGHLIGHTED TEXT:

SNITCHES GET STITCHES

- Genesis 37:2 Joseph's trouble began when he snitched on his brothers. "...and he brought their father a bad report about them." Then jealousy grew (verse 4). When Joseph shared his prophetic dreams about his parents and brothers bowing down to him, he sealed his fate. His brothers hated him and disposed of him in a well.

- Genesis 37:24 It was a blessing that there was no water in the cistern where the brothers disposed of Joseph. He was sold for 20 shekels of silver (8 oz.) and taken to Egypt, where his destiny continued.

reflect

Dare to be different! We are called by God to be different. Joseph could not go with his brothers, not because he was better than they, but because he was doing what was tailored to him – just like his coat! He was placed by God. It was God's purpose for Joseph. Even though Joseph was thrown into the well, he could only "go up" from there! When we are placed for our purpose, we also can only go up!

Even in Joseph's darkest moment, at the bottom of a cistern, there was a blessing. There was no water to drown in; he was in a place where no animal could attack and kill him; and he was in a place where other men would come looking for water. He was found and taken to Egypt. Although Joseph lived through many trying years, he stayed true to his character and to his God, and he eventually gained power over all the land.

Sharing prophetic dreams takes courage, and sometimes, as with Joseph, being a prophet has negative consequences. Joseph had to be courageous. Why would he want to share his next prophetic dream when this first one got him thrown into a well and into slavery? Why? Because God called him to do so, and he answered.

---

respond

How can I dare to be different to be in a better place to fulfill my purpose to further God's kingdom?

Thinking back to the deepest, darkest moment(s) of my life, is there anything about that time (before or after) that I could consider a blessing to bring out of the darkness?

How did God provide for me, even when I didn't realize it?

What problems am I facing this week, and is there any part of the situation that is a blessing or a sign that God is still with me?

resolve

_____

_____

_____

_____

_____

_____

_____

_____

_____

_____

_____

_____

_____

Day 30

read

Genesis Chapter 38

HIGHLIGHTED TEXT:

RESTORING A BROKEN PROMISE

- Genesis 38:15 Tamar is usually referred to as "the prostitute", but she was not a prostitute by profession. Widowed by the death of Judah's eldest, Tamar was given to Judah's second son, which was in accordance to the custom of the day. When the second son died, Judah refused to arrange for her to marry the third son. Tamar, whose only hope was to marry and have children, took desperate measures. She trapped Judah by posing as a prostitute and obtaining his signet ring and staff.

reflect

History would have sounded more honorable had Tamar married Shelah, Judah's third son. They could have continued the family line, as was the custom. Instead, serving as a prostitute, Tamar forced Judah to become accountable for refusing to follow customs and to take care of her as his daughter-in-law. When she became pregnant with Judah's twin sons, Jacob and Esau, the family line was preserved. It is humbling and enlightening to know that the line of Judah was continued through a scandalous scheme of lies, prostitution, and blackmail. Even so, God's covenant with Abraham to have many descendants is honored.

No matter what, everything we break, God can put together. There is nothing too damaged for God. Tamar could still come back, as we all can. Everything has a history, but we can always do better. Anything messed up can be restored with God's help.

respond

Not only does each of us carry on the family name, the family traditions and customs, we also add our own stories to the full history of our family.

How have I added or detracted from my family's history, customs, traditions, and character?

How do I expect my children, siblings, or other family members to carry on the family name?

resolve

_____

_____

_____

_____

_____

_____

_____

_____

_____

_____

_____

_____

Day 31

read

Genesis Chapter 39 & 40

HIGHLIGHTED TEXT:

PROSPERING IN OUR CIRCUMSTANCES

- Genesis 39:2-3 Joseph, living as a slave, prospered and "the Lord gave him success in everything he did." Seeing God's favor on Joseph led to even more success, a promotion in Potiphar's house.

JOSEPH LEARNED FROM ADAM'S MISTAKE

- Genesis 39:9 Joseph was tempted to take the one thing that his master withheld, but he stayed faithful to his master. In verse 12, Joseph leaves his cloak in her hands and runs out of the house....leaving all behind to stay faithful to the master, even if it cost him his cloak and false accusations by her. Yet he was imprisoned as an innocent man, but he continued to prosper because (verse 23) "the Lord was with Joseph and gave him success in whatever he did."

JOY IN ALL CIRCUMSTANCES

- Genesis 40 Joseph meets the king's cupbearer and baker in prison. Joseph begins a friendship with them by expressing empathy to them. Verse 7: "Why are your faces so sad today?" The baker was hanged, but the cup bearer was restored; yet he did not remember Joseph to the king for 2 more years.

reflect

This shows that even though we may be tempted, we can persevere through temptation, and God will honor that. Everybody can be tempted. It's all how we get through and avoid. Even if we fall, God can still pull us back up and we can still prosper through God.

When we know what the outcome is (or should be), the transition or waiting isn't as difficult if we have faith. Waiting without purpose is hard. Waiting with purpose is easier. Abiding in our spirit, abiding in God, i.e. His peace, we don't worry about the "what if's". We simply abide.

Our attitude and approach to life makes a big difference in the outcome. Whether we are oppressed, enslaved, held down in our life situation, we can still prosper by being obedient to God...and authority.

Joseph's temptation by Potiphar's wife is the antithesis of Adam and Eve in the garden. Not only did Joseph refuse to bed with Potiphar's wife, "he refused to go to bed with her or even be with her." He used great wisdom in not putting himself in any situation to be tempted nor to be accused of sinning against God and against Potiphar.

Wouldn't it seem that everyone would seem sad in prison? But not Joseph! This led to his interpretation of dreams. No matter his circumstances, Joseph always demonstrated great strength of character, positive attitude, humility, and empathy.

respond

In what area of my life do I need to consider taking measures to keep myself from temptation, and to keep myself from giving anyone else the opportunity to accuse me of doing anything inappropriate or sinful?

How much does character and attitude affect how I behave in all circumstances?

Even in the worst of times, what can I contribute to positive outcomes and change my life and others around me?

resolve

Day 32

read

Genesis Chapter 41

HIGHLIGHTED TEXT:

TO GOD BE THE GLORY

- Genesis 41:9 The cupbearer recommends Joseph to the king for interpretation of the king's dreams. 41:16 Joseph does not take the credit, but says, "I cannot do it, but God will give Pharoah the answer he desires." To God be the glory!
- Genesis 41:41 Pharaoh puts Joseph in charge of the whole of Egypt to prepare for the upcoming famine, as prophesized in the king's dreams.
- Genesis 41:45 Joseph given a new name by Pharoah... Zaphenath-Paneah to set him up as full authority over all of Egypt.
- Genesis 41:31 Joseph's son, Manasseh is born. His name means "God has made me forget all my trouble and all my father's household. Second son born is Ephraim, meaning "God has made me fruitful in the land of my suffering."

reflect

We are always in some phase of transition. Joseph knew that he would get to where God wanted him to be, as ruler over Egypt. God knew

Joseph would arrive; it was purely God. Giving credit where credit is due, Joseph humbled himself and showed God's personality. God has humility. He could do everything alone, but he does not. He uses people. Putting God first over ourselves means that all the rest will fall into place.

God is humble. God is patient. Jesus humbled Himself to relate to us on all levels. He is not unreachable. We are not unreachable, no matter what we do or who we are. That is the whole point of Jesus' sacrifice on the cross, so that all could be saved.

The cupbearer credits Joseph as an interpreter of dreams. Joseph credits God for the dreams and their meanings. Pharaoh credits Joseph for preparing for the famine and gives him full authority.

Name changes occur again in Scripture, this time from an Israelite name to an Egyptian name as Pharaoh gives Joseph full authority over all Egyptians. Then Joseph names his sons and in those names gives God the credit for his fruitful life.

respond

In my daily walk, how many times do I give credit to God and to others for good things that happen to me?

Do I think that I succeed because of my talents and skills aside from God's benevolence?

When have I taken full credit for some success and neglected to lift up others who helped me achieve that success?

When have I had the courage to give public recognition to God for helping me to achieve a goal or experience success?

How can I make it a habit to publicly thank God and others for the good they have done?

resolve

_____

_____

_____

_____

_____

_____

_____

_____

_____

_____

_____

_____

Day 33

read

Genesis Chapter 42

HIGHLIGHTED TEXT:

THE RIGHT INTENTIONS WITH WRONG RESULTS (DID SIMEON GET IT RIGHT?)

- Genesis 42 Blood ties are strong. Joseph recognized his brothers immediately (verse 7). Simeon sold off his brother Joseph but was detained when the other brothers were sent to bring back Benjamin. Simeon was also the brother but took revenge for the violation of his sister, Dinah. (Gen. 34)

reflect

Simeon is a study of a son who was raised in a spiritual family, the family of Jacob, but makes disastrous mistakes. He could be called a "wild child" in the family. Along with his brothers, Simeon was part of the plot to get rid of Joseph by tossing him in the cistern and leaving him to die. When the brothers were in prison for three days, Joseph wanted to keep Simeon in custody and sent the other brothers to bring Benjamin back to him. Did Joseph intentionally separate Levi and Simeon because of their violence and plundering out of revenge for the rape of their sister, Dinah? Was he trying to reduce the level of revenge that may result from his decisions? They were offered restitution for Dinah, but they chose to slaughter all the men of the town and to plunder the whole city.

Simeon responded in violent ways in revenging Dinah and in disposing of Joseph in the cistern. Perhaps as ruler of Egypt, Joseph want to keep Simeon isolated and contained, away from the rest of his brothers, until the family could be peacefully reunited in Joseph's plan.

In prison, Joseph learned humility. Being away from distractions, Joseph learned. Similarly, Joseph separated Simeon in order for him to be free from distractions, in order to learn and get closer to Joseph and to God. We can separate ourselves for a time from distractions, such as putting our phones "in jail" and away from social media, in order to isolate ourselves from outside influences. In this way, we can get closer to God.

respond

What role do I play in my family dynamics?

Am I considered the "wild child" and reacting quickly and violently when I or a family member is offended?

Am I the thoughtful peacekeeper who plans to resolve conflicts with mercy and understanding?

Who in my family needs extra grace or extra attention to be brought back into the family fold?

resolve

_____

_____

_____

_____

_____

_____

_____

_____

_____

_____

_____

_____

_____

Day 34

read

Genesis Chapters 43 & 44

HIGHLIGHTED TEXT:

JOSEPH TESTS HIS BROTHERS, AND HAVE THEY LEARNED THEIR LESSON?

- Genesis 43   Joseph shows favor to the youngest brother, Benjamin, by giving him five times as much as anyone else's. Judah feels his father's pain in verse 34: "Do not let me see the misery that would come upon my father."

reflect

Favoritism can invite jealousy into the family. Joseph experiences the result of jealousy from his brothers and suffers the consequences of it, as do all the brothers. They took a detour from God's plan for them. Life can get cluttered and messy, but God can restore us all, knowing that we are or will be favored by God. The fact that we are here means that we are favored by God, just in different ways and at different times. Everybody has a designated time of God's favor. God is instilling Himself in us with a plan for each of us.

It is interesting that the brothers "tore their clothes" when harm was about to come to their youngest brother, Benjamin....so different from their response to their younger brother Joseph. Perhaps they learned the lesson of brotherly jealousy, or they respected their father so much as to care deeply for the baby in the family. The brothers had seen their father's misery over Joseph for years!

respond

Joseph shows favoritism to the youngest brother Benjamin, while Judah shows empathy for his father's pain. Is favoritism justified in some cases with some people?

How has favoritism caused jealousy in my family, circle of friends, or in my place of work?

Do I have empathy for others, including my parents, when they are suffering?

Do I know how to show empathy? How?

resolve

_____

_____

_____

_____

_____

_____

_____

_____

_____

_____

_____

_____

_____

Day 35

read

Genesis Chapter 45

HIGHLIGHTED TEXT:

CHANGING THE NARRATIVE

- Genesis 45 Joseph makes God's purpose for him known. Verse 5: "it was to save lives that God sent me ahead of you... Verse 7: "But God sent me ahead of you to preserve for you a REMNANT on earth and to save your lives by a great deliverance." Verse 8: "So then, it was not you who sent me here, but God..."
- Genesis 45:22 Joseph favors Benjamin again with silver and five times the allotment of clothing that was given to the brothers by Joseph. Then Joseph warns the brothers in verse 24, "Don't quarrel on the way!"

reflect

From the cistern to slavery, from jail to Pharaoh's court, every step of Joseph's journey led him to the fulfillment of God's purpose for him: to save lives. The strength of his character and his obedience to God in his most challenging times allowed him to save his life, his family's lives, and the lives of many people. One life lived well = many lives saved!

Finally Joseph is able to articulate God's purpose for him and to share it publicly. He reveals his identity as he "comes of age" in God. Joseph has gone through the process toward his purpose and becomes comfortable in his identity. Some folks still fall toward the world and away from God, but God equips us to that we can withstand the pressure from the world. If we stay close to God long enough, He will equip us to realize who we are and what is our full purpose. That is to advance God's kingdom. Knowing who we are in God means that we also rely on Him timing, not ours.

respond

In my spiritual journey, am I maintaining strength of character and obedience to God on a daily basis, even in small matters or situations that I don't see connected to God's plan for my life?

How is God preparing me in small ways to be equipped to handle bigger challenges ahead?

Am I comfortable with not knowing what lies ahead, only what God has for me to do today?

resolve

_____

_____

_____

_____

_____

_____

_____

_____

_____

_____

_____

_____

Day 36

read

Genesis Chapter 46

HIGHLIGHTED TEXT:

WHEN ARE WE READY TO DIE?

- Genesis 46:28 In the reunion between Israel and Joseph, Israel says, "Now I am ready to die, since I have seen for myself that you are still alive."

reflect

Because we are human, death comes into our minds often, when it will come and how it will happen. It can be scary when we think of our past mistakes. God knows that we would make mistakes, but He knows that we can be forgiven through Jesus Christ. Grace covers us! We can't earn heaven. God knows that we can't pay Him back for redeeming us from our sins. He made a way to restore us through His Son, Jesus.

This is as it should be for each of us as we acknowledge the risen Jesus. Once we have accepted Jesus as our Savior and know that we will live for Him, both on this earth and in heaven, we should be confident knowing that when the time comes for us to die, we will be ready in Christ Jesus!

---

respond

Am I able to say with confidence, "When the time comes, now I am ready to die, since I have seen for myself that Jesus is alive!"?

Am I sure that I will go to heaven when I die?

If not, what do I need to do to get that assurance?

If so, what do I want to do for God while I am still living on earth that will glorify God to advance His kingdom?

resolve

_____

_____

_____

_____

_____

_____

_____

_____

_____

_____

_____

_____

Day 37

read

Genesis Chapter 47

HIGHLIGHTED TEXT:

EGYPTIANS DIMINISH AND ISRAELITES INCREASE

- Genesis 47:18 Representing Pharaoh, Joseph (Egypt) ends up with all the money and livestock..."We cannot hide from our lord the fact that since our money is gone and our livestock belongs to you, there is nothing left for our lord except our bodies and our land." Verse 20 "The land became Pharaoh's, and Joseph reduced the people to servitude, from one end of Egypt to the other..." except for the land of the priests. Verse 25: "You have saved our lives," they said. "May we find favor in the eyes of our lord; we will be in bondage to Pharoah."

- Verse 27: Now the Israelites settled in Egypt in the region of Goshen. They acquired property there and were fruitful and increased greatly in number.

reflect

Because the people realized that their lives were saved, they asked for favor and went into bondage (voluntary slavery) to Pharaoh. In exchange for their lives, he "owned" them. Comparing the people's submission to Pharaoh with our submission to God, we come to the Lord, giving him all that was His to begin with, and we put ourselves in bondage (i.e. complete obedience to Him) to be cared for, to be fed, to survive. No matter what we own or how much money we have, what is more important is to whom we owe our lives. Not the parent or the doctor who brought us into the world through childbirth, not the person who hired us, nor the family member who left us some money, nor even our own hard work. We owe our lives and everything we own to the Lord, who gives us life and salvation through Jesus Christ.

Joseph demonstrates that abilities plus timing equals favor. His brothers also demonstrate this equation. Since they were shepherds, they had the special ability that led to taking care of Pharaoh's livestock. They were prepared and equipped to be favored. God's favor was on His people, the Israelites. They were given a place of promise and peace under Joseph's rule.

respond

To whom do I give credit for my income, my possessions, and my property?

Do I give credit to my company, my parents, winning the lottery, or my work ethic?

How much of myself and my possessions have I "given back" to my Creator and Savior?

resolve

_____

_____

_____

_____

_____

_____

_____

_____

_____

_____

_____

Day 38

read

Genesis Chapter 48

HIGHLIGHTED TEXT:

WHEN WE RALLY

- Genesis 48:2 Israel (Jacob) becomes ill, but when Joseph goes to his father, "Israel rallied his strength and sat up on his bed." Israel restates the prosperity promise to Joseph, and then says to his son, "I never expected to see your face again, and now God has allowed me to see yours children, too."

THE FLIPPED LEGACY CONTINUES

- Genesis 48:14 Israel (Jacob) switches his hands away from Joseph's firstborn Manasseh to Ephraim the younger, just as Israel (Jacob) the younger stole the blessing of Esau. Even when Joseph tries to correct Israel, Israel knowingly passes his blessing to the younger and declares in verse 19 "his younger brother will be greater than he".

reflect

Anyone can carry on a family legacy. God doesn't follow natural birth order but His order for us. Everybody has a different placement of family in the natural, but all of us have a purpose and share in the same family of God.

n Often people on their deathbeds rally when they see loved ones. I, too, have a prayer that God will allow me to see my grandchildren and great grandchildren before I die.

Birth order can determine some personality traits. Typically the oldest assumes most of the responsibility for younger siblings; the youngest often assumes the role of the "baby" and favor; and the middle child struggles to find identity and attention as neither leader nor baby. Contrary to the custom of leaving the family legacy to the oldest male child, we read of many examples of the legacy flipping to the younger, turning their traditions upside down. Regardless of our birth order or favor, God calls each of us to fulfill His purpose for us.

---

respond

How do I relate to members of my family who are older or younger?

Are there different expectations for each one?

How do I relate to my church family?

What am I expected to do to be a contributing member of the church body?

Am I doing what God has called me to do, both within the church and outside of the church body?

resolve

_____

_____

_____

_____

_____

_____

_____

_____

_____

_____

_____

_____

_____

Day 39

Genesis Chapter 49

HIGHLIGHTED TEXT:

THE RECKONING
- Genesis 49 The blessings of Jacob for his sons, the most favorable to Judah, Zebulun, Dan, Gad, Asher, Naphtali, Joseph, and Benjamin. Not so much with Reuben (no longer to excel), Simeon and Levi (cursed because of their anger and fury), and Issachar (forced labor).

reflect

After reading the account of Jacob and his sons, particularly the story of Joseph and his coat of many colors, one might think that Joseph would be the son to continue the messianic line to the Christ Jesus. However, Judah is the son blessed with the line of kings through history. One might also think that the sons would have been equally blessed by the father, as often happens in today's families. However, eight sons receive Jacob's favorable blessings while four receive the opposite, i.e. curses. There is good reason for Jacob's decisions. Firstborn Reuben defiled his father's bed (49:4); the next in line, Simeon and Levi demonstrated uncontrolled anger(49:5);

Joseph continued to be highly favored (49:22-26); but it was Judah (a middle child) who was chosen to be a father of future kings. Once again, birth order did not turn out to be a birth right. Each son was judged and blessed or cursed based upon on his character and his actions, and these blessings and curses filtered down through the family line.

The sons had an idea, an expectation, of being blessed by their father. God had other ideas for each of them. We can't determine our own outcome by what we see in ourselves, but by what God sees in us.

---

respond

Can I identify types of blessings or curses that I seemed to have inherited through my family line?

If I were to be judged today with blessings or curses based upon my character and actions, what might I expect from Father God?

What have I done, and what have I become, to be looked upon favorably or unfavorably by God?

What might I want to pass on to my children, my grandchildren, or to my community of believers during my lifetime?

resolve

_____

_____

_____

_____

_____

_____

_____

_____

_____

_____

_____

_____

Day 40

read

Genesis Chapter 50

HIGHLIGHTED TEXT:

- Genesis 50 Joseph grieves for his father Jacob for 40 days for the embalming process, and Egyptians mourned for 70 days. Jacob is buried near Mamre. Genesis 50:20 Joseph to his brothers, "You intended to harm me, but God intended it for good to accomplish what is now being done, the saving of many lives. So then, don't be afraid. I will provide for you and your children." And he reassured them and spoke kindly to them.

- Genesis 50:24 Joseph reminds his brothers about the prosperity promise from God to Abraham, Isaac, and Jacob.

- Genesis 50:26 Joseph was placed in a coffin in Egypt.

- The book of Genesis has traced the family tree from Adam to Jesus in the designation of the messianic line leading to Jesus Christ. Genesis has also given a detailed account of God's covenant with His people, from His promise in the Garden of Eden to His promise to Abraham. We have read how the Israelites came to be in slavery in Egypt, and we have seen how all actions have consequences, even as God's purpose for His people continues toward fulfillment. The Book of Genesis has set the foundation of the earth and of heaven, the covenant between God and His people, and the journey to seek and to wait on the Messiah to come. Exodus, the next book of the Bible, takes us further through the Old Testament as people wait for the Messiah, breaking and re-establishing their part of the covenant with God several times. Only the New Testament when we read the account of Jesus, the Messiah, being born, will we see that the struggles and the wait was worth the coming of Jesus, Savior to all who call on His name.

reflect

Joseph didn't know exactly what was going to happen, but he did know God and trusted in Him. He trusted his prophecies given to him by God. Genesis wraps up a final thought that brings Joseph full circle, from his natural father's favor to his heavenly Father's favor in his words: "You intended to harm me, but God intended it for good."

Genesis shows us that from the beginning, God has purpose for us. We are created in God's image, and God says that creating us is good. The following chapters of the Bible show us how God leads His people to their purpose, to their identity as people of God.

Today is only the beginning of where God is going to take each of us in our lives.

Joseph was buried near the place where God spoke to to him, where he had experienced the closest intimacy with God. Joseph was in the place where God had raised him to prosper and to save lives.

---

respond

If I were to plan my own funeral today and wanted my body or my ashes to reside in the location that meant the most to me in terms of my closest times with God, where would that place be?

What places and times stick in my memory that designate proof that God speaks to me or that God hears me?

Where do I go to hear from God?

Where do I go to speak to God?

resolve

_____

_____

_____

_____

_____

_____

_____

_____

_____

_____

_____

_____

_____

Conclusion

After weeks of reading Genesis and talking together about our reflections, Francesca and I realized that we continue to seek God through the Word and through our idea of what it means to be created in God's image. This is only the beginning. Now we forge on to Exodus to see how God continued to guide, correct, and save the people of God, despite the poor images of disobedience and rebellion. We will also see Godly images of great leaders and warriors who heard God and stood firm in their calling. We are reading our family history of the good and the bad, and in all of it, we find our image through God and our identity in Jesus Christ. We know that when we read Revelation, the final book of the Bible, we will see the victory and triumph through Jesus Christ and all promises of God fulfilled, as promised from the very beginning in Genesis.

Thank you for reading along and participating in our 40-day look into Genesis. Not only did Francesca and I learn more about each other in our discussions, we learned more about ourselves. If you love the book of Genesis as much as we do, you can study more in-depth through books and commentaries from notable theologians. If you love to continue reading and responding to the next book of Exodus, we are right there with you! Enjoy! Be blessed!

CPSIA information can be obtained
at www.ICGtesting.com
Printed in the USA
BVHW090904160921
616887BV00015B/402